Saraswati's Lament

Poems from Bali

Barbara Roether

Wet Cement Press
Berkeley, California

Copyright© 2019 Barbara Roether
All rights reserved

ISBN: 978-1-7324369-0-9

Wet Cement Press
Berkeley, California

www.wetcementpress.com
wetcementpress@gmail.com

Cover image: The yantra, or divine
diagram of Saraswati

Special thanks to my friends in Bali, Sinta, Ari, Mahmud, for leading me into the garden of Saraswati. And for my San Francisco family, holding loose and tight.

WCP1-1

Contents

A Foreword with Notes on Balinese Sources	vii
Nyepi: Words from the Day of Silence	1
Prologue to Beginning	10
Arrival	14
Offering #1	16
Offering #2	17
Máde	18
Bird Taxis	20
Longing	21
Always Kites	22
The Witch's Deal	24
Talking Fire on the Island: An Homage to Frank O'Hara	25
Capitalism	30
Om, Money Come to Me	33
Her True Colors	34
Women Love Who Listens	41
Prambanan: The Ruins	46
The Fish Asana	49
Nasi, the Rice Goddess	51
Nightmares with Skype	52
Trunyan Cemetery	55
Swimming Holding Hands	58
Ahmed on the North Coast	59
What I Learned from the Dalang	60
Coffee with Buddha	62

Jalan Drupadi	64
In Hong Kong Airport	66
Saraswati's Quintet for Winds	67
Three Poems with Butterflies	70
Four Sonnets	74
The Sound of Him	76
About the Author	81
Wet Cement Press Titles	83

A Foreword with Notes on Balinese Sources

Periodically I like to leave. It is as if I am called away. This collection was written during a year I spent teaching in Bali. My husband stayed in San Francisco, my son went off to college. I knew that I was coming back. Still, there were difficulties that I was trying to get away from, and trying to get to. We travel to arrive.

In Bali, Saraswati, the Hindu Goddess of poetry, music and learning, is honored on every street corner. You can tell the shrines that are dedicated to her because they have swan wings on the back of the stones. Where I lived in Seminyak my crowded street (or Jalan) was named for Laksmana, the hapless brother of Rama, whose story, the *Ramayana*, is woven throughout the Hindu culture of Bali. Images from this epic, along with some Indonesian folk tales, and the *I La Galigo,* a 14th century epic poem from the island of Sulawesi, are also woven into this work.

In Bali every child can weave a palm leaf tray at the age of seven. Weaving is everywhere—ancestors into relationships, religion into daily life, the unspoken into the spoken. Stories also weave together the Hindu, Muslim, and Buddhist cultures that are the actuality of life on the island. Borders, where one set of beliefs begins and the other ends, are fluid. Each claims the other as its own relative. Everyone participates.

Through the turning of the year, the sumptuous round of Balinese sacred days and ceremonial rituals, suggested structures for these poems; especially the Balinese New Year, Nyepi, or the Days of Silence. Quiet is the mother of all poetry.

for Mark
Om Swasthi Asthu

Nyepi: Words from the Day of Silence

Prologue.

In a Balinese gate
there are two sides
as if split in half
and a wall set straight ahead.

One may pass to either side
but cannot enter in a straight line
because as everyone knows
demons can't turn corners.

Knowledge of demons
guides us.

I.

I am returning my body
to the flavor of beginning.

There is a breeze rising
tomorrow is Nyepi the Day of Silence,
the New Year.

Is writing keeping or breaking silence
    pen skimming across the paper
motorcycles across the road
dragonflies in the yard
a history of alphabets

Balinese scripts no longer used
left lying like twigs on the grass
the breeze again.

Where is there silence
in this world
the buzz of our knowing
colors everything
as blue does the sky.

II.

Last night
burnt offerings
fires at the gate
of each 'gang' or gateway
flames carried out by grandfather grandmother
small children trailing behind
with the wooden clacker
to scare off the demons
bundles of twigs
or torches of tar bearing the flames
as night slips through
the barricaded streets along
Jalan Kerobokan
the Ogoh Ogohs*
are lined up on their bamboo platforms
demons fallen from the sky
borne through the avenues
giant horned demons swaying living,
edged under the electric wires over the street

sparking on contact
their bleeding mouths
engorged penises
pendulous breasts
fangs dripping red, or white
sperm or blood.
In the night before the silence
inside us or
outside us.

III.

Woken in the night
by thunder and lightning to see if any rain
is pouring into the room filling it
with water or with liquid light
but no
the room is still empty.

IV.

Nyepi Morning
On this Day of Silence
humming of the insects
but somewhere still a hotel generator
whining of the engines we have made
louder than living things.

V.

Time now to prepare the offerings
for my doorway

and the temple in the yard
with flowers purchased in bulk
at the Sukawati market
returning via motorbike from Ubud
   with Samantha,
we stopped among the thronging women
buying hundreds of offering trays,
kilos of flowers in plastic bags, bales and
   bushels
of silken petals
golden, scarlet, magenta, white
this glut of beauty
the weight of it
feeds us.

At the kitchen counter I take red pink
   purple golden
flowers in a square palm leaf tray and
   sweet grass
to add to the center
put on my sarong and sash
take them to the shrine in the yard.

Offer
my hesitation
my shyness
> for at such unfinished edges the spirit
> catches hold.

VI.

The rooster calls out the swelling day
clouds block the sun.
Afternoon, in the green yard
sound of purple jacaranda flowers
the quiet increasing
can quiet increase?
Swelling at its center
until
something is born
we are able to hear.

Oh Saraswati so much of what
comes to mind to say
is in answer to what is said
how can I remain with the world
& learn to speak from
the center of an
original flower?

Light shifting into late afternoon
or early evening.

I have been a scientist of light
its slant in rooms
have I captured any
shadows, curtain
pulling this now a
luster reflected from the white paper.

VII.

Chanted Chenresig
nothing was said
to anyone
only you
future reader
(meeting in a distant silence).

Dark now
no lights allowed
I am writing by cupping my hand around
a small candle
the island finds its true darkness once more
and I find the blackness wherein
all my habits are stacked thick and tattered
like old offerings from which the essence
has been taken but not the origin

bright green of the baskets rotting into brown
and soon the rats

is there a
can I find a
truer light?

VIII.

Past midnight of Nyepi

It is said the evil spirits are passing

above the island now
and seeing no lights, never bother
to stop.

They are not the smartest spirits apparently
and I wonder why if a spirit can't be seen
can it only see things that are visible to us
wouldn't it have awareness of what is hidden?

Such logic is useless here, like
coins from another kingdom.
But the sky wearing all its stars
is visible over the tourists tonight
the still water in the abandoned pools
at the W Hotel
will reflect their glory.

I walk outside to see
the street with no one in it
there are penalties for being out
but wonder is stronger than fear.
(There are two white teenagers skateboarding
down the middle of the street,
I yell at them, "Have some respect!"
"We do this every year!" they shout back.)

IX.

The Day After Nyepi

This day receives the quiet

closed silence
of yesterday
now opening to receive
another sound
still quiet around the edges
a kitten mewing
the air strangely clear
the nature of quiet
emerges gently
as a child's nature emerges,
after birth without words but
in the particulars of his glance.

In the yard
red of the hibiscus, sings open
stepping stones set off against
the greener green
of the grass.

—

> Nyepi, the Lunar New Year, is celebrated in Bali in late spring. There are several days of processions and prayers; on the second day the electrical grid is basically shut off. Radio and TV stop broadcasting, the airport is closed. Tourists are restricted to hotel rooms. Residents devote themselves to self-reflection and meditation. Pecalong, or ritual guards, patrol the streets and make sure no one is outside. The devout will cook

meals ahead of time so no fires are lit, as fires are known to attract demons.

*Ogoh Ogohs are effigies of gods, demons, and mortals created to celebrate the New Year. Each neighborhood competes to make the most amazing figures which are destroyed at the end of the week.

Prologue to Beginning

*I pray that my prayers and offerings
are well received, just as they are intended**

I.

It was as if she had swallowed a seed
grew inside her
until it was larger than her mouth
like a mango's white moon
she couldn't spit out
whatever fruit this seed encased

*Transforming knowledge, on this earth beneath
the sky.*

You've already made up your mind to go,
her husband said.
Though she feigned innocence
could not with any sincerity argue
one journey chosen for herself alone
perhaps she clung most
to the power of her choosing.

On this earth beneath the sky.

What could she say
their marriage was like
fishermen with old boats,

lines cast into the deep
they always needed money
their son was going away to college.

They were living by the beach at the edge
of San Francisco where the city
disintegrates into sand blew everywhere
it was so foggy and cold no one wanted to visit
it was disheartening
as if that were the best weather
they could ever hope to afford
constant growl of the ocean
across the Great Highway
one day a whale carcass was washed ashore
red blubber flesh carved into cliffs
and mountains
redolent of other worlds.

She asked her son
what he thought of her leaving
though he was leaving too,
"I think you should stay with Dad"
sitting in the soft chair in the kitchen,
while she cooked meat for him at the stove
not even the voice of her only son
could stop her
not even meat or a child.

Flower offerings completed the shaman's ceremony.

Even to herself she could not say
why she felt so determined to go
walking along Ocean Beach
searching for the phrase an ocean mumbles
what we are beyond this shore
what we do when left to our own

not that either

I go far away
because there is
always a distance
inside of me
I go to meet

the distance.

You were called the Unopposable One.

II.

She flew there in an enormous night
ever westing into
the Pacific Ocean of all hours
future and past
across the
Mother of all Nights
Mata Malam.

Inside the body of the airplane
she huddled
like one who has been swallowed
by a beast of the deep
her cheek against the cold ribs
of the black window
searching.

Through darkness I came
The gates to the sky were opened wide.

...

And a bamboo raft descended
Upon which Batara Guru lay.

---

* Italicized sections from *The Birth of I La Galigo* ©2005 The Lontar Foundation.

Arrival

Near dusk
a rainstorm
soft on the mango trees
then louder
just before dawn

after the rooster
the dog
some passing music
on the street beyond the walls
it must be gamelan
gongs, loud banging
I go out to see
but it is
already gone

this life will have to have me
for I have forsaken all I had
to come to these empty rooms
in a dark hour

have I sinned against love
packed paltry possessions in a suitcase
but left what was tender

beets in the garden
they were too small

a deep scarlet
with griefs buried
in their round root.

Offering #1

Alone here to begin with
I am left with myself.

What is the noise
made by time passing?

Each place speaks
its own dialect of light and shape.

Bali, if I take your words
I will give you mine

leave them here
in shallow baskets
woven of palm
with nine grains of white rice
upon a dark green leaf
offered at a thousand shrines
I do not know the meaning of

but I know the meaning
of offering.

Offering #2

In the broken shade
against the hot white wall
of the Circle K convenience store
the young street woman
who sells the woven bracelets to the tourists

nurses her child
her naked breast is large and full

how the breast fills for the child
despite the thinness of the mother

the meaning of offering
latched on.

Máde

Every morning at seven
like bird song
Máde
calls up softly
(in case I am naked)
hello
he is coming upstairs
barefoot silent
with offerings for the shrine
in the corner of the living room
smiling in his pink sarong
he sweeps in,
plume of incense rising
from the tray
above his head
flowers rice
water
wands
words

a gecko lives in the shrine
and eats
whatever he leaves

the gecko is a goddess
too.

—

The corner of my living room is the southwest portal of the property which belongs to the protector gods. Although within my apartment, this is also considered a public space. Concepts like public or private have little meaning here.

Bird Taxis

How they were here all along
the taxis painted with blue birds
driven by men in blue shirts
not driven by birds but
so what if they were?
We could learn to accept that too.

Do we contain each place already?
Is being new to any country
about having to remember
what it was we've forgotten?

Take us back to the beginning
the scent of cloves
hunger of temples
hollow interiors
the end of Ramadan
the start of Galungan
tiles awaiting tiles
on rooves
awaiting rain.

Longing

All over this country stone-carved
shrines
guarded by intricate demons
their round eyes bulging
gates that stand open
waiting for someone.

I miss my child
my husband
or is this simply
the eternal longing
of being
little breeze
between the wood-frame windows.

My heart is as the shrine
in the bambooed corner of the green yard
a location I am called to
but cannot enter
verdant stalks too dense for passage.

Always Kites

What is there always

there is always light
doing something
and the sky
though not always blue.

Always there is an ocean
like this one
a man on a wave
a girl with a surfboard tanned skin
pausing to watch
always there is a story you are part of
and another story
you don't understand.

Always there is a moneychanger
currency passing through hands
always a mother whose child has gone
a river of weeping where her child used to be
always a city
stairs leading to doors
always a key is needed
construction workers
barefoot on the bamboo scaffold
building hotels for strangers
always someone is coming.

Always here
there is
a black kite in the sky
shaped like a ship
and other enormous kites like vampires
or clouds
rattling in the wind.

Always there is
a cat looking in the window.

Always there is grain ripening
rice fields greening
always cloth strung on wires
to keep the birds away
an old woman hiding in the straw hut
in the middle of the field
will come out
momentarily to shake the wires
that hold the cloths
that scare the birds
away.

Always they come back.

The Witch's Deal

The cat
is my suspicious solitude
an umber-colored creature
of long-legged cut
youngish by her lithe step
stub-tailed
not a single cat on this island has a tail
    victims of some secret tragedy
    a witch's deal gone cheat

how long does evolution need
to shape appearances?

from the couch I call to her
but she stays in the kitchen
jumping from counter to floor
and back silently

she will not come to me
or I will not
come to myself.

Talking Fire on the Island:
An Homage to Frank O'Hara

There's no one to talk to here
but I need to talk exchange
ideas with everything
in desperation
I go shopping
hoping against hope this hot
grimy night and emptiness to ignite
some satisfaction.

I buy a long red skirt
think look my hips are on fire
I have a long red skirt but
I still can't shake this wandering
around Bali's dark broken sidewalks
glass-fronted boutiques and the
muttering retreats
of shop girls kneeling over cell
phones in the air-conditioned
cubes
whispering to men or mom
because no one ever comes in
so I go in.
Come out keep walking
down the busy darkness
night falls
soon in the tropics
like a mildewed tarp from the sky.

Usually the tourists walk so slowly
hesitantly
I walk into the streets
    to get around them,
an ambulance
swerves to avoid me and my emergency
in a hurry to get somewhere
but where, where is it we keep
racing around for
is it a story using us
a song this walking is the melody of?

Across the street from
Máde's Warung a man is tearing down
a stone wall
hammering against the stone with
a chisel and his lifetime
while some Balinese dancers in their
flowering heads and gold-wrapped breasts
dart across the alley on gamelan feet.

I stop at a little restaurant called Zulu
the anorexic girls in the next booth are saying
"Don't you feel like this year has gone by
quickly?"

No I don't I am
in a slow fire of longing it seems
like I always have been
but of course I don't say that

I want to say
my hips are on fire
I am full of desire
I bought a red skirt
but those are just lines
the trouble like always
is in a restless mind.
At night on Seminyak Avenue
a hundred people walking by
the satay man at his grill
transforming flesh the black
smoke of death fresh coriander
his yellow dog, its spiral tail.

Who reads poems anyway
I am jealous of Frank O'Hara
who was allowed to talk
to the sun on Fire Island,
I am on an island
and would love to talk to the sun
or moon
or anyone for that matter
but no one shows up.

In the daytime cats come
into my flat
but they never let me touch them.

So I take to the streets looking
often I am happy and peaceful
but not tonight it is hot
in this vast living room (home now)
in bra and shorts
sometimes it seems
the only time I can remember
not feeling lonely
is when I was making love
or writing poems
and then I felt really connected
it's not subtle I know.

I used to have a lot of sex
but not so much anymore
sometimes I see beautiful young men
walk in, like at the restaurant tonight
and it takes me a while
to remember how old I look now
it's shocking really.

The Pema Chödrön engagement book
lying on the desk
offers more days of emptiness
just to taunt me.

I still prefer the living
lotus flowers
pale yellow
in the stagnant trash-strewn pond

down the block from here
floating just above
the algae-covered scum
in bold and curvaceous
yellow coronas of perfection there are
a hundred lotuses
triumphantly alive.
Which is all I can say tonight.

Capitalism

My son at university in California
proclaims
across the great distance
he is studying the rise of capitalism.

I take a walk
along the broken sidewalk
on the street outside my house
a trench is being cut along the curb
by hand with shovels
the pavement peeled back
like a scab
revealing the gray
volcanic earth beneath
boys in waist-high water all day all week
digging out a vein for water to the new hotels
or somewhere else the riches run
away from their labor
in dark veins
beneath the surface

while tourists above them
in perfumed throngs
loosed
from cool hotel rooms
flash
diaphanous silks
and stumble stork-like

on silver platform sandals
chattering where to eat tonight
any of these passersby
could look down

to see these thin men
in the gray wet channels
below their feet
every twenty yards
a naked brown back
painted with the chalky ash
rippling muscles
taut with strain

like a cursed fetus
in a dark hag's womb
one boy, too long in the slop
his hands, swollen like coral reefs
held up to show
an older man must be his boss
only shrugs.

Oh thin men of Java
what sin was yours to show us this circle of hell
Dante wrote of long ago
how the lucky step on the heads of the cursed
or a local custom called 'toil and suffer'
not mentioned in any guidebook

and no one at all
among the tourists who pass
pauses to look down at the humans below
afraid to see
what they have not been told

this monstrous oblivion
what bought and who sold?

—

> Rampant hotel construction across Southern parts of Bali have decimated the natural resources and polluted the environment. Threats of social unrest and calls for a moratorium on hotel construction go unheeded. Javanese Muslim workers occupy most of the construction jobs in Bali, as they are cheaper to employ than the Balinese.

Om, Money Come to Me

Even sanctify the shops of
alcohol and whoredom
tonight at the glinting chrome and red wine bar
that opens onto the street
a purification ceremony
is spilling far into rush hour
street clogged with growling motorcycles
pyramids of offering fruit,
mango, guava, palm weavings,
the fat priest in white sweating and
the horns honking
as the traffic struggles to go around
(we've walked by so often wanted to drink there
but couldn't for the lost looks of the girls
barely teenagers, dressed up like toy soldiers
in black boots, scarlet mini-skirts,
low-cut brass-buttoned jackets
standing outside at all hours)
the liquor bottles above the bar
caught in the mirror of
shining golden twilight
the priest chanting
money, money,
buttocks, breast.

Her True Colors

> When I heard the Indonesian folktale, *Joko Tarup and the Rainbow Angels*, a tangled piece of my marriage suddenly seemed clearer. The mysteries of the feminine lurk inside this story. I wanted to play with that strand, and invent some others, about what women give, and how men receive it.

I.

With a wind that scattered leaves, the color angels came down from heaven. Appearing unexpectedly as rainbows always do, trailing color. They came to bathe in the fresh water of a clear lake, ringed round with lotus flowers that floated like tiny temples.

Unwinding their red orange yellow blue green indigo and violet sarongs from just below their breasts where they had been so tightly sashed they were relieved to breathe deeply, and lift their bangled arms to unleash their hair which fell like flowered bouquets to their rounded hips.

(Indonesian angels have no need of wings, since they use their sarongs for flying, though you wouldn't guess that by the way they threw them in a sloppy heap under a tree by the shore.)

"Oh that feels better," said the yellow fairy her
brown nipples shaking as she strode into the
water, the others followed "ah," they sighed
diving into the deeper water, (very deep
waters) then surfacing like sea otters they
played, floating soaking, it was a hot day. Even
in heaven in had been too hot.

II.

And of course a man came along (as you might
have expected) his fields were nearby but he
had never seen women like these. Never even
imagined. He watched them from behind the
jacaranda tree his cock stiff and his eyes wide
open.

He saw their sarongs flung at the base of the
tree picked up the green one, the color of
new rice, silk it was and his roughened farmer
hands snagged it as he stuffed it in his pouch.

The women were coming out of the water. He
wanted to see but he was afraid. He ran away
into the bamboo.

The angels still dripping with water and
laughter came onto the land, after sitting for a
moment in the sun to dry slid fresh frangipani
flowers behind their ears, began to dress,
wrapping themselves in their vivid sarongs,

except for the green angel (her name was Nawang Wulan) who for some reason could not find hers.

Maybe it was simply blending into the grass, suggested the blue angel as hers was often lost in the sky. She tried to help but the orange angel, always ill tempered, was in a terrible hurry to get back (to what though?) and scolded her saying, "We shan't wait, you're so scatterbrained. Find it and then come, no point in us all waiting here by this dreary little backwater."

So they put on their sarongs and taking the edges held them out behind them then rising past the palm trees, past the mango past the giant black kite whistling in the sky, vanished.

Nawang sat with her back against the tree weeping, her clothing, her wings, her home all taken at once. Something touched her shoulder and she screamed. "Don't be afraid," said Joko Tarup, "Are you lost?" "That's the understatement of the century," she replied. "Who are you?"

He explained, "I am a farmer..." (who hasn't had a girlfriend in many years but he didn't say that) She explained what she had lost, he seemed slow to her, but she wanted to be kind.

He studied her beautiful eyes, emerald green, her glossy hair, it was late afternoon, time ran slow, the heat was dense, her body so naked, nothing or many things happened, then a bird sang, signaling that they were married and she had gone to live in his house.

What choice did she have, he was handsome enough, his chest firm and brown. He had some substance, unlike the boys she knew in heaven. When his fish swam inside her, she laughed, then their son was born. Joko was incredibly happy, not only did he have a son now, and a beautiful wife. she was also an incredible cook.

It seemed they never ran out of food, the bags of good red nasi rice stored in the loft overhead never seemed to get smaller. Even when the locusts came and the neighbors' ribs stuck out Joko's house had bags of rice still waiting. He even had enough to sell, and still they always had more. How did she do that? He wondered for a minute, then just stuffed his mouth with more nasi, fish, duckling. He started to sleep on the couch all day, went to shadow puppet shows all night.

One day he was home, lounging on the bále when Nawang wanted to go out and gather some snake fruit or salat. She said, "I ask of you only one thing my husband, when I am gone. Please do not look in the cooking pot."

No sooner was she out the door and down the path... He really shouldn't have done that.

It's not what was in there, one grain of rice on the bottom, which mystified him, it was...

When she came home with the salat and a long branch of rambutan, saw the lid all askew, she knew right away, she felt what he had taken.

After that each day Joko saw their rice supply was dwindling. He went out to his fields frantically, planted, though the harvest was still far away.

One day in that season Nawang went up the narrow stairs to the rice loft, lifted the last small bag of rice from the wooden floor, mice scurried, chaff rose in the air like butterflies, and there in the spot where the rice bag had lain, she saw a smaller thread-worn pouch, she put her hand inside it, felt a cloth, pulled it out. It was her green sarong, memories of the lake came flooding back to her.

Then she knew.

When he came back from the fields stinking of dead fish she said, "Joko Tarup, you took my freedom, though I did not know that, and I was willing to give it, but then you questioned my gift, and so by questioning, ruined the magic by which I kept us. Am I not allowed to have anything of my own? You've betrayed me from the start. This was my secret and not for you to have.

You need to understand about women, Joko, that their generosity is endless but let them give it in the way they will and never question the nature of their giving, as if the gifts are not of her own making but they always are. What they give is always on purpose, never by accident, as you have been to me. "Anyway, Joko, I'm out of here."

"No, no, please Nawang I love you," (he really did love her he just wasn't that smart). "We have a child, you can't leave our child." (That did get to her, but the boy was old enough now). "He can call out to me if I am needed and I'll come to him."

She wrapped her green sarong below her breasts, tied it firmly with her sash.
"What do you mean," he was saying "please don't leave me, I...." But before he could finish his sentence she flew out the window.

Women Love Who Listens

> In the *Ramayana*, Rama's wife Sinta, is famously
> kidnapped by the demon Rawana. Rama has to
> find a way to rescue her though he's a bit slow.
> Hearing the story in Bali I sensed the secret power
> of another character, the bird Jathayu, the one
> who notices what is amiss. Jathayu, is the husband
> women long for, not a god-like hero, but a
> beautiful bird, with excellent hearing. Women love
> the one who listens.

I.

As Sinta peeled her sweaty cheek from Rama's
chest and rose to dress, she noticed, feeding
near their hut, a delicate fawn. How its
golden coat caught the sunlight like a clear
water stream. Rama, look! How gorgeous is
that fawn, she murmured in her sultry voice.
I'll get it for you Rama mumbled, though
Sinta didn't mean that he should get it just
that he could notice it's beauty, but they were
both young and though neither said so, they
were aroused by the idea of the hunt, the
grasping of the writhing flesh, the binding of
the fragile legs.

II.

Sinta insisted Laksmana go too, he was
an idiot and she wouldn't put up with his

gawking at her all day. It was good to have
some time to herself. She loved living in the
jungle though she knew better than to say
that to Rama. It was hot and she laughed to
herself as she stripped her sari off once they
had gone. She tied it around her waist so
she could walk more easily. She felt proud
of her muscled calves now, the rounded
hardness in her arms. With each breath she
inhaled the humid incense of leaf and rot.
She never missed the palace with all its rules.
She walked into the streams, splashing on
purpose, crossing over the rocks, swimming in
the deep pool at the feet of the banyan tree.
Then stepping soft on the musk litter of the
forest floor, warm sun through the leafery
casting a green light on it all. Sinta loved the
wilderness in her heart. She sat by the stream,
her legs folded beneath her watching who
came there to drink: a weasel, cranes, a tiger
once who saw her but only growled softly,
dragonflies of a deep red hue.

III.

Some hours passed and she wondered when
Rama would return. But could also imagine
living without him. She wondered sometimes
if this was wrong, how easily she could
imagine life without him.

IV.

She knew there were other kingdoms his mind traveled to. He would speak of Ayodhya and wonder when he could reclaim his throne, as if the throne of love he had so recently, and readily, mounted was not enough. What is this desire in men for the world, she asked as the banana leaves rattled, and she wandered the landscapes of her own mind like an ancient fisher gathering her thoughts silver-schooled then scattered up from the deep.

V.

When would the men return? They really should have been back by now. Rama is a pompous fool, she thought. He had to go capture the deer to impress her, and leave her alone so he would have to find her again. But perhaps love needs to lose and find. Women must disappear so that men can follow. It gives them a sense of purpose. Even I can see that, thought Sinta. Then a lightning bolt lit the western sky, and cold raindrops fell.

VI.

Back in her hut, she dozed, waiting. Another crack of lightning hit the hut and there was a loud knocking. A low voice pleading, "A monk in need of shelter please?" And even as she opened the door, even as before her eyes Rawana changes from a tiny yellow monk to the fat red-eyed demon he always was, even then, she thinks, Why did I ever think Rama would protect me? No one can protect anyone. Then Rawana caught hold of her, lifting her into the air, with no consideration of the pain of his claws in her thin bare shoulders, and the blood trickling so dark over the rising of her collar bone, the disgusting gore caked about his tendons, and the stench of dead things from his black sarong. And her stiff breathless fear, as she is pulled through the air high above the palm trees, over the undulating jungle, holding on, helpless, unseen. She calls out.

VII.

Alert in the understory, Jathayu was listening. His iridescent emerald neck turns to hear her call. A woman is calling, he knows this song. His great wings spread open, and with a whipping roar, like a sailing ship on water, he soars upward toward the dark shape of his destiny. Nearer he recognizes Sinta, and she calls out to him, "Oh Jathayu help me!" (As if he could, or any bird, save a woman married to a conceited prince from the arms of vengeful demon, but he tries.) And Sinta's heart is healed with love for the world, that it contains one so attentive, so brave, who swoops in close when it is hoped for the most, out of the clear blue sky.

VIII.

Rawana saw Jathayu rising then dropped suddenly, swooping down like a heavy gong, as his claw cuts the jugular vein on Jathayu's turquoise neck. Sinta and Jathayu looked into each other's eyes in mid-air, in mid-time, blue green his feathers, his round eye black. He falls, broken-winged a rain of red blood scattering like petals of hibiscus, crashing through the coconut palms to the ground where he lies, crooking his neck to staunch the flow of blood. He holds fast to the sentence he will say, must say. Lives on the minutes of his intention. When Rama comes looking he will tell him. Will Rama come looking?

IX.

Then footsteps are near, Jathayu hears him striding through the grass, sees his feet, his ankles wrapped in gold lame. Rama stops and bends near. "Jathayu what has happened to you?" Blood in the words pouring from his mouth, "Rawana has Sinta!" And his beak then not closing. Who loved her more? The man who ran looking for what he wanted her to have, or the man who heard what she needed?

Prambanan: The Ruins

> Near the city of Jogjakarta, (Java's old capital), lies
> the ancient Hindu temple complex of Prambanan.
> Its three stone towers, massive and intricately
> carved, rise fountain-like from the valley floor. At
> night the towers are lit as the backdrop for a dance
> performance of the *Ramayana*, which occurs
> in a large outdoor theatre just across the river.
> Tourists can meet the different characters in pre-
> show events, where actors pose for pictures like
> at Disneyland. I saw Rama there, and as with the
> Jathayu story, heard a different telling.

I.

Gede has played Rama for sixteen years, his
feet deformed with calluses a slight limp
when he's not dancing, young men strut to
the back stage door their bodies round and
smooth, how boldly they knock asking to
audition, everyone wants to play Rama but
what do they know of exile and failure? From
what wound will their arrows fly? Still he
knows any day now.

II.

Every night he fights Rawana as if to defeat
him, and all of time. The other dancers
complain his steps are too erratic, when he
twirls the sword, it's frightening, he shoots

the wooden arrows right at us, someone will
lose an eye, it's almost as if, (according to the
pudgy 20-year-old who plays Rawana) "he
really wants to take us out."

Of course I do, Rama thinks to himself,
and will before this drama's done. So far the
manager shushes them, but for how long?
The old are brave in a way the young can only
imagine.

III.

At the ticket gate he takes his turn posing for
photos with the Australian tourists who know
of the story only that there is fire in the third
act and monkeys.

His friend Laksmana speaks gently, "Look
Gede, at this photo, people complain. The
deep wrinkles in your face show through the
golden makeup up close, it startles them. Your
costume is worn and tattered that tear in your
leggings, sewn badly people want the smooth
illusion."

He is thinking of the repairs needed, tiles
falling from the roof at home, how the
forehead of his youngest daughter burned this
morning, dengue fever.

They won't replace his costume and he knows why. They are sewing a shirt for a different chest than his. Too many seats go empty each night.

The managers take the money.
People have no patience for epics.

He's heard the other dancers gossip, "Rama's not pretending, he's gone over!"

On the stage Rama's armies form and disperse, one battalion green, the other yellow, one leg of the dancers always raised to the side, a crab-like stride, the monkeys enter with a simian slouch, a warrior lunge, brocaded sarongs snag the light spread and swarm, spinning like the stars overhead.

In the third act, the accustomed fire of the final battle overflows its bounds, catching several costumes by the hem, (shouting, water, foam) then the wooden bridge to Lanka, flares.

The arena lights are turned up, the stage manager comes onto the floor with a loudspeaker to guide evacuations. But just behind him against the gathering smoke, Rama keeps dancing.

The Fish Asana

Everywhere here there is yoga
as there always has been
my teacher Putu
is a good man
his name means first born
I am secretly in love with him
his clean white clothes against his dark skin
he is Shiva,
my intimate brother.

In the warm dark
something new in my body answers
his voice
you have known this breath before
it sighs inside you
in muscle and bone beyond wanting
your knee, shoulder, folded waist
a constant child explores
inside the body's blood-dark pulsing.

Then lying prone on the smooth cool wood
Putu names the parts
of the body
become his voice
in a Balinese accent
count the joints
to the right nostril
middle of the eye to the left nostril.

It is hot in the studio
night falls through the windows
shaped like stars
motorcycles hum
on the street below
right elbow
forearm to wrist
to the palms to the thumb
pointer finger, middle finger
to the palm to the wrist
repeat on the left.

And to the chest
to the throat
and always the word throat
transformed in his saying to "trout"
the fish
suddenly vivid there
silver-skinned
russet-flecked
flickering up the windpipe stream
from the depths of my body
from the trout to the mouth
pointed toward my lips
emerging
airborne
birth by words
to sound the shape
of being here.

Nasi, the Rice Goddess

In the afternoon
longing for greenery

I ride my motorbike to Umalas
the district at the edge of town
where a narrow raised roadway
cuts between two rice fields

today two women in straw volcano hats
are working at the harvest
stooped among the bundles on the roadside
they are throwing the rice from their baskets
up
into the winnowing wind
    then laughing with abandon
        as the chaff snows down
            on their heads and shoulders

How golden are the cut stalks still standing
and the smell of the field
so pungent
with what has been given.

Nightmares with Skype

I.

When I Skype home
and see my husband's face
I cry unexpectedly
because he has a body
but I cannot touch it.

My son is there too
bare-chested and tan
watching the two of them
sitting in our bedroom, the unmade bed
wind lifting the Indian print curtains I chose,
it is as if I have died
and I am watching them
go on without me.

II.

This distance from my son plagues me
like a troublesome dream
and there were so many
when he was small,
    always a thin child,
    light enough to carry on a hip
    up to seven or eight I felt
    the frail lengthening branches of his bones
    the memory of the angle of his shoulder
    blades

    like wings, closer now
    than the distance that holds us apart
Even then dreams held him apart from me,
night terrors they called them
I'd find him crouching in a corner,
his mouth stretched in a grimace,
his cheeks wet with tears
pleading with the fanged demon,
that held him in its grasp
trembling with fear, his fists fiercely clenched
a ragged ancient warrior, inside his tiny limbs,
his look of beleaguered suffering,
never forgotten.

Even as I took him into my arms, said
"it's just a dream,
it's not real," stroked his sweating brow
"momma's got you now,
there's nothing there, it's just a dream."

"Look, the fire in his mouth," he'd whimper,
"it's burning!"

I felt the terror, in the presence of his seeing
felt but could not see, the snapping black dogs,
fire-breathing lions.
"No, there is nothing there," I chanted
fear pumping through my blood
"there is nothing there," I said
but knew there was.

Sometimes it took five minutes of pleading
until recognition lit up his eyes
and he would embrace me.
I would give him a drink of water
as if the clarity of water could rinse the stain
carry him back to his bunk bed
and thinking it had passed,
lay down beside him.

Then pouncing out of the shadows
again the black dog, snapping at his face
"Help me, help me!"
and I am next to him, searching
crying now too in desperation
looking around the room
the dog in the night wind, beyond my reach

until waking him again,
    as from the first awakening
which is only the dream disguised as waking

my child would return to me.

III.

I am so hungry, he says on Skype.
I get up to make him something, but then remember
the ocean in between.

Trunyan Cemetery

I.

South of the equator
we live in an inverted night
is like day
dreams possess a perfect logic
while waking is a puzzled trance.

Yesterday out walking
I saw a fire inside of a coconut husk
    (smoking to keep the mosquitoes away)
my skull is a coconut husk,
my dreams smoking embers.

Dawn amidst the mosquito nets around the bed
like fishing nets, my body caught from
the ocean depths, washed ashore.

Here days lounge warm around
without edges
smoke of clove cigarettes
the ceiling fan's orbit
another cremation procession
gamelans clanking
on the street below

what is clear in the darkness
hidden in the light

how things burn.

II.

Today
my friend Dana calls
she's just gotten back
from taking her students
to visit the graveyard at Trunyan
near the volcano Kintamani
where bodies are simply left to rot
under a giant banyan tree
said to absorb all bad odor.

She told how
the children picked up the bones
played with them
skulls
and femurs they held aloft like clubs

(were the bones dreaming, pleading
in the hands of the children "Oh give me
your youth, your young flesh again?")

"You let them play with the bones?" I asked
"No one cared," she replied, confident with the
Cleveland country club she came from.
Some Americans are ruined for reality.

How could a deeper instinct not warn her
I would never have allowed
my students to touch the bones
belonging as they did

to someone else and all the places
where they walked all in that bone.

III.

A few months later
Dana will kill herself
I don't know why
or if she meant to
she was living in Virginia then
in a dark valley
photos of the house looked slanted
I didn't ask her daughters for details
not wanting to picture
her remains.

She was a good friend to me
so searching for reasons as one does
remembered her saying
"I thought moving to Bali would make me
a different person."

At the time I didn't answer
but I should have asked
who
who is it you want to become?
And are you her now?

Swimming Holding Hands

Near the reef
I hold Ari's small fragile hand as we
snorkel
in the shallow warm water
    she is Balinese this is her island
    she is young
    has never gone snorkeling before

take her small fragile hand
lead her into
    the water that is hers
how tiny her wrist is in mine

joined this way we swim
across the fantastic coral
striped zebra, clownfish

she was proud when she lifted her mask
"I saw the fish, so beautiful!"

I hold her hand in the ocean
though the ocean belongs to her
in letting me guide her
gives it to me.

Ahmed on the North Coast

In the tiny fishing village
of Ahmed
time grows shy
we watch
the flying fish fly

Above the rippling surf
fuzzy stuff of the kapok tree
skids across the sky blue
boats on the horizon
painted pink and green
outriggers bent like giant insect legs

For lunch we eat eternity
caught a moment ago
from the deep
it tastes slightly salty.

What I Learned from the Dalang (The Shadow Puppet Master)

The tree spins out
from the light
bright void
flickering
falling
toward the earth

roots the sunlight to ground
stabbed deep into the banana stem
along the base of the Wayang Screen

> theater of being
> where dark shapes of our journey
> show against an amber sail.

This is the tree at the center of the world
Gunungan,
no story can begin without it.

This is the tree of talking
every shape grows on it
the screen is your dream
the screen is your skin
the screen is your paper
waiting for a story

an alphabet of postures
the puppets remember
who we were to begin with.
Every life a shadow
playing
on other lives
degrees of transparency
weights of darkness
how we touch.

Coffee with Buddha

Writing at the Anomali Café,
where the coffee is a young intellectual
elixir of sunlight and Hindu incense
with dark notes of fruited volcano
and sacramental shade

liberation is near or far

across the blacksilver river
of roaring motorbikes
on Jalan Laksmana,

a giant pink plastic Buddha sits
with his hands folded,
peering patiently through
the tarnished picture window
of the expensive gallery

every day I feel for the Buddha
locked in there, the indignity of pink plastic
the dirty window
though of course he knows more than I do

liberation is far or near

stray yellow dog with a spiral tail
moves in the heat

a Japanese woman all in gray
reads her Japanese novel with a gray cover
exotic only means distance
what we have pushed away from ourselves
when we get closer, all is familiar
in the nearness of being

liberation is.

Jalan Drupadi

The simple presence of the world
how the grass drinks in the rain
the rooster's message
watch which direction the wind comes from.

Walking
along Jalan Drupadi
    street of the goddess of a thousand saris
when her captors tried
to strip her naked
found only more saris
under her sari and
under that one
yet another
spinning without end.

Deep within words
there are alleys

paved with stones
along one side the water flows
in channels you walk beside
listening to the flow

high walls, against the channels,
behind the walls
and hidden in the trees,

villas
where carved lions
their mouths agape
guard the portals

these are words there are
alleys in words
where
children on motorbikes race
carrying brooms to sweep the
school
while old women gather piles
of the fallen brown withered
frangipani petals
to press for oil

listen.

In Hong Kong Airport

I.

Used to a warmer climate now
not shy of shadows found
what it was I
in some deeper country thought.

II.

I don't know anymore about religion
that old Catholic priest at auntie's
funeral who said
efforts made on behalf of those
you were closest to
was as much as.

III.

Just now a monk
or a man in monks' clothing passed by
walking extremely fast
at first I thought
this amazing pace must be the result
of some spiritual training he had undertaken
but then I realized
he was on the moving walkway.

Saraswati's Quintet for Winds

I.

Returning to Bali
sitting in the blue interior
of the watchful taxi
taxi taxi
I say "Meter please."
Let's count the miles
until we are wind.

II.

Is love in the grasp of time
woven of afternoons
the first kiss in the car on Broadway
illicit feet under the table
at the publisher's lunch
driven by flesh
to share a bed a life
shafts of light
blowing in through the eastern window
blue gray glowing
outline of a bending tree
within the frame.

III.

Winds gather
like threads
with which to weave the evening
crisscrossing

cooling
restless
as language is

above the corrugated metal roof
the mango tree
heavy with green globes
periodically the ripe fruit
    falls
        thundering down
scattering the cats in the yard

what was speaking.

IV.

Still the west wind
for the third day
gusting and twirling through the green
garden
as if this wind was all our thinking
restless saying, no,
but must
stems release leaves
still hold, still cling
can quiet come
why wind
what is it wanting
why mind needs to
ravage the edge
of every standing thing
banana leaves torn to a perfect fringe.

V.

Next day
no wind
the feast of Saraswati begins
at every temple
pyramids of fruit
towers of woven stars
flowers, suckling pig
her feast but the men preside

fat priest in white, late for the engagement
cigarettes in his tight breast pocket
he rings his bell chanting
    but a woman makes the offerings

this ring water from green coconuts
this ring incense
this ring flowers pink purple red and gold

scattered from the
bunched leaves of mango
water perfumed with jasmine
    poured into the cupped hands
to the mouth to the hair
then choosing a flower from the basket
holding it between the two first fingers
above the forehead like a steeple

we enter
    the flowering
church of ourselves.

Three Poems with Butterflies

I.

Wind of the monsoon's arrival
blows through the windows
of sleep

a wet sprinkling along
arm and cheek
its cool presence welcome
like someone we are longing for
entering from the dark veranda

where earlier this evening

I saw two black butterflies
in a double dance
only courtship could conceive
one butterfly mirroring
each V and veer of the other
moving it seemed, in knowledge of the others
motion before the other even
identical darting
spiraling, wings opening
hovering, over the spider lilies
black letters typewritten on white
paper erased or already received
occupying, momentary
locations in air the other had just

still I am filled with wonder
can this be common (do lepidopterists know?)

our longing to join
or already one?

dark scripts of unity
the presence
of
yes.

II.

On the stairs that descend
the carved gate of the old palace in Ubud
the dancers descend
in blazing brocades of
green
    pink
gold
staccato steps feet bare feet
crowns and jeweled hair quivering
rain of gamelan hammers falling down
heels descending lift and beat

it used to be the dancers
were all prepubescent girls,
and before that they were little boys
disguised as little girls
and before that they were firelight
now they are dancing kupu-kupu tarung,

the dance of butterflies
the wings on their
hands find some flower in the darkness
to touch
in the dark musty heat of the courtyard
thunder roaring from far away
hammer on wood, footstep on stone,
one music
the gamelan like flames, raging smoldering

everywhere bodies in motion's time,
and the circling of earth
dancing a sentence we cannot say only
    move with
into and out of this light.

III.

In Ubud
returning to the hostel
after the Legong dancers
quiet
late at night
shops empty
locked against the hour
I see through the glass
of an empty white jewelry shop
a black butterfly
against the white tiled floor
trapped
fluttering

in the brutal brightness of the flat
fluorescent light
alone there
jewel-like its flutter dark shine
opening closing
only my eyes
witness
who can I tell
the black butterfly
is trapped
in the white jewelry store

each heart
contains the same

call the owner
open the door.

Four Sonnets

I.

Here there are no seasons
but the fluctuation of my longing
the sharp catch in the chest
one man in whom my heart rests
I long for him as bird for nest.

II.

In those we love our lives are larger than now
lit from within as wick to oil
as root clings to river through
the dense intention of rain
pouring against tile rooftops.

III.

He is rain to me
shower to ground
greening leaves bathed and fresh
as my skin would be if only he
pressed down from above.

IV.

Plumeria trees in the wind
shadow limbs against the white sheets
of the morning laundry

In a week I will be home
to visit

my husband loves me
to be loved is the fruit of living

Write him a note:
"Soon I will come to you
You are the country I call home
the only place we can lose ourselves
is where we are already known."

The Sound of Him

I.

After five months away
I can no longer remember
any of the problems
I had with my husband

or why I left him over there

Peace has settled in
the ocean between us
our pirate ships all sunk

We speak every morning
    his voice a warm gulf stream
have a great deal to say
he collects stories brings them to me,
like bouquets on the balcony
news of the world, San Francisco, Paris, Arabia,
I put them in vases around my solitude

How
by taking everything else away
come back to what
it was I loved
to begin with
his voice

II.

Now while he is
hidden from sight
I find like the blind
other qualities more acute
    my hands remember
the tenor or tremor of
his body folded
and carved inside his voice
old stone dark lichen and crumble of days
past tangible
open as gates to the temple are
always open

so when I touch his body again
my hands will find
the day we first touched

his voice containing
the shapes of all we've held
    rising like islands in the sea of our living

our place on Shotwell Street
the first time in Big Sur, the waves below
    the balcony
the taste of lemon tarts
desperate for water in Morocco
the voices of our little boys deepening into men
and the girls who came near them to listen
a snow-drenched tree we admired in Yosemite

when he dove naked into the pool in Puerta Vallarta
and the waiters threatened to send us home

but they couldn't because
we were already going.
I circle the world
to hear
his voice more clearly

when we were young
so much in love like an eternal sunburn
on Broadway in SF, right down by Battery
where we used to park to kiss before work
how long ago the car was light blue, a Valiant
it stormed every night we made love
the first month
it was always 3am and El Niño
couldn't sleep for the magnetic pull of him
a constant tension along the skin
as if awakening to
what had been before, had it?

Love has no boundary
and I have measured it to make sure
the width of the Pacific
turning south at Taiwan,
descending
below the equator
into dreams,

and how it rained.

About the Author

Barbara Roether is a writer and teacher recently exiled from San Francisco to Asheville, North Carolina, where she now hosts a literary reading series. She is the author of the novel *This Earth You'll Come Back To* (McPherson & Company) and a poetry collection, *The Middle Atlas*. She frequently reviews books, and writes of faraway places whenever she can, a travelogue of Japan is forthcoming. For many years she worked in book publishing as an editor and created the series *Signs of the Sacred* with Harper Collins Publishers. There is more information on her website *BarbaraRoether.com*.

Wet Cement Press Titles

Series 1

My Dog, Me (novel), Anthony Schlagel
ISBN 978-1-7324369-3-0 (2019)

Saraswati's Lament (poetry), Barbara Roether
ISBN 978-1-7324369-0-9 (2019)

Synonym for Home (poetry), Michelle Murphy
ISBN 978-1-7324369-2-3 (2019)

Wilson Wiley Variations (poetry), Thoreau Lovell
ISBN 978-1-7324369-1-6 (2019)

www.ingramcontent.com/pod-product-compliance
Lightning Source LLC
Chambersburg PA
CBHW060502080526
44584CB00015B/1517